HISTORY AND PHILANTHROPY
PAST, PRESENT AND FUTURE

EDITED BY
DAVID CANNADINE AND JILL PELLEW

Published by

Institute of Historical Research
School of Advanced Study
University of London
Senate House, Malet Street, London WC1E 7HU

ISBN 978 1 905165 32 2

Contents

Introduction

David Cannadine and Jill Pellew

An important role of the Institute of Historical Research is to provide the historical context for activities that are key to the functioning of modern society. There is no doubt that the subject of philanthropy – historical accounts, current practices and future directions – is of immense interest today. Individual contribution of money, time and involvement, in order to ameliorate core areas of social need, has been a leitmotif of civilisation. This critical aspect of civil society is currently under the spotlight because the need for philanthropy is as great as it has ever been. Governments are facing enormous challenges from new directions that can only seriously be addressed with philanthropic input. At the same time, in recent decades there has been a huge surge in private fortunes. Indeed, we have been in the greatest age of fortune-making since the late nineteenth and early twentieth centuries; and the present scale of wealth is unprecedented. This combination of urgent need and the acquisition of immense wealth are naturally inspiring many global conversations about philanthropy.

This IHR seminar on *History and Philanthropy: Past, Present and Future*, held in London on 13 November 2007, focused largely on the arts and humanities. Its object was to initiate dialogue among historians, donors, practitioners and fundraisers – in other words, to bring together people in the philanthropy sector some who have worked on its history, some who practise it now, and others who are speculating on where it is going. Included in this publication are the papers (by Jill Pellew, Frank Prochaska and David Cannadine) for the first session of the seminar that were intended as historical vignettes about philanthropists from different eras when the accumulation of substantial wealth made significant social changes possible. The story of sixteenth-century founders of Oxford and Cambridge colleges, as much as that of the legendary Pittsburgh millionaire and founder of the Washington National Gallery of Art, Andrew Mellon, points up some enduring characteristics of major donors to education and the arts: their intense engagement, enjoyment and generosity in the process of giving. The narrative about new Victorian methods of delivering relief and other blessings to those in need illustrates how ongoing engagement with philanthropy impinged on all levels of English nineteenth-century society almost as an industry.

Also included in this volume is the introductory paper (by John Tusa) for the second session of the seminar where debate was focused on philanthropy today and its possible direction. This led to a subsequent panel discussion by a distinguished group of current practitioners from both sides of the Atlantic (Bill Dietel, Beth Breeze and Theresa Lloyd, chaired by Barry Supple). Short papers by these contributors to the panel session can be found on the IHR's website and are an important complement to the articles included here. Whether or not philanthropy is old or new – a question which, in itself, probably does not get us very far – some interesting points emerged. We are now in a world where not only is there more money than ever before, in terms of large fortunes, but these have been globally derived in a way that simply was not true before. While old Europe and the United States were once the main sources of wealth, now fortunes are coming from China, Russia, South Asia and the Middle East. Thus the sources of mega fortunes are much more varied than in any previous era. The natural concomitant of this is that the focus of many of these people is global. They are concerned with world problems: AIDS, global warming, poverty in Africa. And some of them certainly seem to want greater control of the use of their fortunes on this considerably greater canvas. Part of this control lies in a private sector approach to the way in which their investment is managed.

The issues towards which today's major philanthropists often direct their wealth tend to be medical and social. The other side of the coin is that there is a lacuna in the channelling of great wealth towards the humanities and the arts. How should those whose passion and work lie in these sectors convey their needs to those able to make a real financial difference with major private investment? The challenge here may be to engage with these people in a way that convinces them that interaction with outstanding museums, with top quality music and with the best historical teaching and research can have valuable social repercussions worthy of the enthusiasm, involvement and generosity that has characterised great philanthropists throughout history.

New philanthropists of the Tudor period

Jill Pellew

The sixteenth century was a golden age of benefaction to Oxford and Cambridge universities. Between the founding of Christ's College, Cambridge in 1506 and the completion of the Bodleian Library, Oxford in 1602, major donors founded or re-founded 14 colleges and two major libraries, and established many public lectureships and professorial posts – not least the five Regius chairs – at each university. These spectacular developments were the backdrop to the transformation of the collegiate universities into cohesive, national institutions.[1] Within this period an interesting phenomenon occurred: a change in the nature of benefactors. Until the momentous sequence of events surrounding Henry VIII's divorce from Katherine of Aragon that led to the Reformation, founding colleges had often been the business of a Church that was responsible for promoting the education of its monastic and secular orders. The early sixteenth-century founders – the pious Lady Margaret Beaufort, Bishops John Fisher and Richard Fox, and Cardinal Wolsey – were excited about new humanist ideas which led to important changes in the curriculum and a greater emphasis on preaching. Yet they continued the tradition of the great prince bishop founders, starting with William of Wykeham in the fourteenth century. From the mid sixteenth century, in the years following the break with Rome, the baton in the race to augment the educational facilities at Oxford and Cambridge passed from the Church to men who were benefiting both from the decline in power of the great bishops and from service to the Crown.

By the mid 1530s, Henry VIII badly needed money for an ambitious foreign policy. This had to be financed through a mixture of taxation, loans, depreciation of the coinage and the sale of property. Crucial in the tale of the founding of Oxford and Cambridge colleges was the sale of land following the dissolution of the monasteries from 1536 onwards. By 1547 the Crown had received about £1.5 million from the sale or leasing of monastic property; and it continued. This vast release of landed property onto the market had the effect of enriching a new group of professional civil servants whose skills were needed in the management of Crown finances. At the same time, the Crown's need for ready money, through major loans, enhanced the careers of merchants and city businessmen. An important group of Oxford and Cambridge benefactors, who had profited through these economic and social shifts, decided to leave their mark on the world through major donations to higher education. This article addresses the following questions about six of these men: who were they? what were the relationships among them? how did they make their fortunes? what were the motives for their major donations? what were their methods in promoting their institutions? what was the outcome of their benefactions?[2]

Four of these benefactors made their careers and fortunes working on the administration of Tudor finance and were each particularly connected with the workings of the Court of Augmentations, set up in 1536 by Thomas Cromwell to administer the transfer of monastic property to the Crown.[3] They were Thomas Audley, Lord Chancellor to Henry VIII and founder of Magdalene College, Cambridge in 1542; Thomas Pope, Treasurer of the new Court of Augmentations, and founder of Trinity College, Oxford in 1555; William Petre, privy councillor and Royal Secretary to several monarchs, who effectively re-founded Exeter College, Oxford between 1566 and 1568, with the endowment of eight fellowships; and Walter Mildmay, Chancellor of the Exchequer to Elizabeth I, and founder, in 1584, of Emmanuel College, Cambridge. Two others in the group of 'new benefactors' were Thomas White, senior Merchant Taylor, Lord Mayor of London and procurer for the Crown of large-scale loans and support from the mercantile community, who founded St John's College, Oxford in 1555; and Thomas Bodley, who served as Elizabeth I's Ambassador in the United Provinces and created the great Oxford library between 1598 and 1602. These six men spanned a period of roughly two generations (Audley died the year that Bodley was born).

These men tended to have come from relatively humble origins (Pope the son of a yeoman farmer, White the son of a modest clothier, Mildmay the son of a Chelmsford mercer). As for their education, four of them, Audley, Petre, Mildmay and Bodley, had studied at Oxford or Cambridge colleges. Two of them, Petre and Bodley, had spent part of their youth on the Continent, and consequently became fine linguists. The other two were not university-educated: Pope was articled as a young man to a senior Crown official; White began work as a merchant's apprentice. Our six benefactors rose to prominence and attracted the attention of the Court in different ways. Audley was an able parliamentarian who became a close ally of Thomas Cromwell in the execution of the Reformation legislation and succeeded Thomas More as Lord Chancellor. Pope was attached to Audley's household before rising through various clerkships in Cromwell's civil service to the treasurership of the Court of Augmentations.[4] White, whose early apprenticeship was to a well-known member of the Merchant Taylors' Company, soon rose to prominence as a merchant and leading member of the company, and was thus an obvious channel in the securing of major loans to the Crown. Petre, an Oxford tutor to the brother of Anne Boleyn, went abroad in the service of the Boleyn family and thus came to the attention of Henry VIII. Mildmay's brother-in-law was auditor and councillor to Katherine Parr. His elder brother was already in the Court of Augmentations and paved the way for his becoming an auditor there where, as an exceptionally able financial administrator, he quickly attracted the attention of Sir William Paulet, a senior privy councillor. Bodley (much younger), valued for his linguistic ability, become involved in affairs of state in his late 30s under the patronage of the Earl of Leicester. All six men were knighted for their services to the Crown. Only one – Audley, who became Baron Audley of Walden – was ennobled. They all made money and died substantially richer than they were born, having secured a higher social niche than their fathers.

Their lives intersected at many points. Within the small circle of senior officials focused on the monarch and Court, with the possible exception of the much younger Bodley, they must have known each other well. Audley promoted Pope and must have been responsible for his rise to a senior position at the Court of Augmentations. Audley decided on the re-foundation of his former Cambridge college within two years of his death, and bequeathed endowment for its transformation into what became Magdalene College, nominating Pope as executor of his will. Pope and White, founders of adjacent Oxford colleges in 1555, were friends who shared Catholic sympathies. Audley and Petre were neighbours both in the Aldersgate Street area of the City of London[5] and in the country in Essex. Petre's long career as a senior administrator, under every Tudor monarch from Henry VIII, also bought him into close contact with Pope. Petre's life was similarly intertwined with the life and career of Mildmay, another neighbour both in London and in Essex. Both these men were involved in the surrender to the Crown of the great abbey of Bury in Suffolk in 1539.

Table 1   Major Tudor foundations at Oxford and Cambridge

Founder/Benefactor	Foundation/Re-foundation/ Other benefaction	Date of Benefaction
John Alcock (1430–1500) Bishop of Ely	Jesus College, Cambridge	1496
Lady Margaret Beaufort (1443– 1509) Mother of monarch + John Fisher (1469–1535) Bishop of Rochester	Academic posts, Oxford and Cambridge Christ's College St John's College, Cambridge	 1506 1511
Sir Richard Sutton (c.1460– 1524) William Smith (d.1514) Bishop of Lincoln	Brasenose College, Oxford	1512
Richard Fox (1447/8–1528) Bishop of Winchester	Corpus Christi College, Oxford	1517
Cardinal Thomas Wolsey (1470/1–1530) Royal Minister	Cardinal College, academic posts, Oxford	started 1525
REFORMATION	***Dissolution of monastic houses***	***1536 onwards***
Henry VIII (1491–1547) Monarch	Regius Chairs, Oxford and Cambridge Trinity College, Cambridge Christ Church, Oxford	1540 1546 1546
Sir Thomas Audley (1487/8– 1544) Lord Chancellor	Magdalene College, Cambridge	1542
Sir Thomas Pope (1507–59) Treasurer, Court of Augmentations	Trinity College, Oxford	1555
Sir Thomas White (c.1495–1567) Lord Mayor of London	St John's College, Oxford	1555

Dr John Caius (1510–73) **Physician**	Gonville and Caius College, Cambridge	1557
Sir William Petre (1505/6–72) *Royal Secretary*	Endowment of eight fellowships to Exeter College, Oxford	1566, 1568
Hugh Price (*c*.1495–1574) **Treasurer, St David's Cathedral**	Jesus College, Oxford	1571
Matthew Parker (1504–75) **Archbishop of Canterbury**	Personal collection of books and MSS to Corpus and Caius colleges and to University, Cambridge	1574
Sir Walter Mildmay (?1520/1–89) *Chancellor of the Exchequer*	Emmanuel College, Cambridge	1584
Lady Frances Radcliffe, Countess of Sussex (?1531–89)	Sidney Sussex, Cambridge	1596
Sir Thomas Bodley (1544/5–1613) *Diplomat*	Bodleian Library, Oxford	1598–1602
Sir Thomas Nevile (*c*.1548–1615) **Dean of Canterbury**	Great Court, Trinity College, Cambridge	1595–1605

Italics indicate 'new men' who made their way in the service of the monarch.

They also jointly re-founded Chelmsford grammar school, following their official involvement in the dissolution of several local schools under the Chantries Act, and both their families continued to maintain links with the school foundation. Mildmay was a mourner at Petre's funeral.

The middle years of the sixteenth century remained an age of faith: it was a time when royal servants could be executed for politico-religious failures; it was an age of religious martyrs. Yet in the post-Reformation years there appeared a new phenomenon of professional men who had the skills – financial understanding, languages, administrative drive – to provide the Crown with the civil service it required to develop a new, more secular state. These men acquired an additional talent – that of being able to serve a variety of different political masters – which foreshadows the more modern British civil service. Pope, Petre and Mildmay, who lived and worked through the tense years following the break with Rome, all managed to serve the Tudor monarchy right through the religious vicissitudes of the turbulent middle years of the century without seriously affecting the continuity of their careers.[6]

The most graphic example of this is Petre, described as Catholic by inclination, but for whom professional success – and its concomitant accumulation of great wealth and all that it brought with it – was what really mattered, not faith. Petre, by 1567 'the sole relic of Henry VIII to attend Elizabeth I's Privy Council', was the arch trimmer, a man who 'always cultivated the art of survival'.[7] He had played a prominent, seemingly ruthless role from 1536 under Cromwell, in the visitations and spoliation of religious houses all over the country. When Cromwell was in trouble over the marriage negotiations with Anne of Cleves, Petre (who had been deputed to be part of the negotiating team) adroitly managed to escape the mission that led to Cromwell's downfall, which Petre therefore survived. Under Edward VI he became sole and senior Royal Secretary (which position he held until his retirement in 1557) and in the final days of the young King's reign drafted some of the documents altering the succession in favour of Lady Jane Grey, to whom he actually swore allegiance. Despite all this, like some other councillors he changed sides when the tide quickly turned in favour of Mary's succession, and he soon became a senior adviser to the new Queen who may have warmed to him because of his family's sympathies with Catholicism. He entertained her at his Essex estate, was closely engaged in negotiating the marriage with Philip of Spain and maintained ongoing links with the Spanish King. Petre played a definite role in the ruthless Marian burning of heretics, many of whom were torched to death in his county of Essex.[8] It seems likely that he was assiduous about this matter more through his professionalism as a civil servant than on account of his Catholic sympathies (though his wife's strong Catholic instincts may have influenced him).[9] He continued as a member of the royal council, though with less influence, in his declining years under Queen Elizabeth, whom he also entertained at his country seat.

By contrast, Walter Mildmay was always clear about his sympathies, which were firmly Protestant, if not puritan. As a result, he did not prosper politically after the death of Edward VI. However, his fiscal and general administrative talents were such that even in the Catholic reign of Mary, his skills remained in demand and he participated in many special commissions before Elizabeth's accession, when his career really took off. He did not disguise his deep convictions from the new Queen, for example when the French duke, Alençon, was courting her, which he believed seriously threatened the Protestant settlement. Yet he remained *au fond* 'the queen's good servant ... not an uncritical servant, nor as we might say, his own man so much as a man who lived to serve the commonwealth'.[10]

Any great era of benefaction depends on a surge of wealth, that not only generates the capital necessary to found new institutions, but also makes men optimistic and generous about extending their vision far beyond the requirements of their immediate dependants and social networks. This surge in the mid sixteenth century was provided by the dissolution of the monasteries. All monastic estates were released to the Crown at a time when the royal coffers were haemorrhaging the fortune amassed by Henry VII to support a foreign policy that involved a series of military engagements in Scotland and in France. Thus many of what first became Crown estates were soon put on the market and often re-sold, during an era of rising prices, which obviously benefited those who were able to sell on. Most of the monastic estates were sold at a standard price, fixed by the government and universally applied to all buyers. But the Court of Augmentations provided the perfect vantage point for making fortunes. In 1540, Thomas Audley was granted the sinecure of High Steward for the Court of Augmentations of all lands formerly belonging to religious houses north of the Trent. Through buying and selling he was able to build up a substantial estate, largely in his own locality of Essex, that included the former Walden Abbey – the source of his family estate and thus the title of his barony. Pope, who is described as a 'frenzied' buyer and seller, in 1547 acquired a former grange of St Alban's Abbey, Tyttinhanger in Hertfordshire, for his country estate.[11] When he founded Trinity, Oxford in 1555 he claimed to hold 27 manors in seven counties, and at his death his bequests included extensive estates in Oxfordshire, Hertfordshire, London and elsewhere. Petre, who was involved in monastic visitations right from the start in 1536, equally bought and sold on a large scale, amassing substantial landholdings in both his native west country and around his newly acquired locality, Essex. For his country seat he chose the manor of Gyng Abbess, formerly owned by Barking Abbey, granted to him by the Crown and renamed Ingatestone Hall. Mildmay was appointed in 1545 Co-auditor for the Court of Augmentations for Cambridgeshire, Essex, Hertfordshire, Huntingdonshire, Middlesex, Norfolk, Suffolk and London and subsequently (like Audley before him) for the area north of the Trent. A man of probity, who, it was said, refused to enrich himself, Mildmay nevertheless acquired his country seat of Apethorpe in Northamptonshire while building up the fortune he was later able to use in the endowment of his college. His estate was estimated at £20,000 at his death.[12]

In addition to these property transactions, public servants earned good salaries if their fees and perquisites are included. Audley's high stewardship of all the Augmentation lands north of the river Trent, for example, netted him £100 a year for life for virtually no activity.[13] Petre received an annuity simply for being in attendance on Queen Mary when Philip of Spain arrived. His steward's records of his annual accounts show that his income from salaries, fees and perquisites rose steadily from £109 in 1540 to £2,719 in 1570.[14] Mildmay, who was awarded a generous pension for life by Mary following work he had done on a financial commission, became 'one of the most highly paid Elizabethan officials receiving salaries, pensions and emoluments of as much as £500 a year and perhaps that much again in fees'.[15] Bodley acquired significant income from his diplomatic role in the United Provinces.

There were other sources of wealth available too. Petre, for example, married a rich widow from his neighbourhood who 'brought with her a healthy portion of £280 a year'.[16] Bodley was the only one of these benefactors who was, from the start, financially independent through his family and he was therefore able to spend some years travelling before entering the Queen's service. He later received a generous inheritance from his father. Meanwhile, he had married Ann Ball, daughter of a Bristol merchant and widow of a wealthy fish merchant from Totnes in his home territory of the west country. Wealth from trade, from which Bodley partly profited, was another significant factor in the story of the Oxford benefactions, notably in connection with White and the founding of St John's. Like other successful London merchants, he made his fortune through risking investment in diverse overseas trading ventures such as the Muscovy Company.

What, then, were the motives of these benefactors? Whether or not an individual was personally pious, religion, with its wide implications of extensive social duty, including the promotion of education, was highly significant. Pope, White and Petre were most naturally in sympathy with Marian policies and understood the requirement for an educational bulwark in support of the battle against heresy. Founding Oxford colleges, in order to provide a stream of properly educated graduates to fill clerical and administrative roles, was a splendid way of meeting this need. In the case of those 'new men' who had made their fortunes out of the destruction of their inherent religion there may have also been an issue of conscience. Pope and Petre were entranced by the acquisition of wealth and the material trappings that it brought to them personally. Petre, who seems actively to have enjoyed the work of plundering the monastic estates he

inspected, was certainly not spiritual. When it came to serving a queen of
their own faith in 1553, neither of them cared to risk losing his new found
acquisitions. Indeed, Petre went to the length of securing a personal papal
bull confirming his property rights.[17] Yet Petre was from a Catholic family
and had a devout Catholic wife. It is quite possible that his benefactions to
Exeter College, and equally his previous work setting up the new grammar
school in Chelmsford, were partly expiation for the ghost of a major sin.
Pope is described by a contemporary as 'a perfect catholic'; and certainly
the statutes of Trinity, Oxford 'revealed a strong religious motivation and
enthusiasm for the rites and ceremonial trappings' of the Catholic Church,
not least in the purgatorial aspect of prayers for the founder and his wife.[18]

Mildmay, on the contrary, a 'deeply convinced, unbending Protestant',
founded Emmanuel, Cambridge a generation later, specifically in order to
establish 'the godly preaching ministry'.[19] Based on the model of Christ's,
an earlier foundation, his mission was the conversion of all of England
(later New England) to the Protestant gospel. Mildmay's faith had an
ethical dimension in the context of the way in which he had made money
– through the destruction of monastic property. He was professionally
and personally concerned for the proper dispersal of the spoils and (as we
have noted in the case of Chelmsford grammar school) pressed for their
application towards charitable and municipal uses such as the re-founding
of schools formerly supported by chantries and poor relief.[20]

Mildmay was exceptional in this group of college founders in another
respect: he deliberately did not make provision for the education of
founder's kin and young men from the founder's locality. With the other
benefactors this sense of duty towards family and locality, as a motive for
their foundations, was striking. Ring-fencing places for founder's kin, as
scholars and fellows, was standard practice in the case of all Tudor collegiate
foundations, many of whose statutes followed earlier models in this, as in
other practices.[21] This could prove problematical: the poor initial President
of Trinity, Thomas Slythurst, found it exceedingly difficult to meet the
requirement of his patron, Pope, that the 12 fellows should have been born
in the founder's own manors or otherwise in counties where he owned land.[22]

Three of these men – White, Mildmay and Bodley – had a passionate
vision of what they wanted to achieve with their benefactions. They,
perhaps, were less involved in the business of creating a dynasty (White and
Bodley, indeed, had no children) and leaving their fortunes to their heirs.
Rather, during their lifetimes, they committed a large part of their fortunes,
and in the case of both White and Bodley much of their later lives, to their
projects. For Thomas White, imbued as he was with the philanthropic

traditions of the London guilds, the founding of a new Oxford college was part not only of a religious endeavour, but of a wider educational vision designed to improve the lot of young apprentices. Acutely aware of industrial social and economic problems affecting his trade, this creative benefactor used his wealth to fund a series of schemes, culminating in a project, centred on Bristol but involving 22 other urban cloth-making towns, administered by the city leaders and designed to provide long-term, interest free loans to young apprentices, preferably in the clothing industry. The principle was that White provided a large sum with which the city fathers could purchase land (some of which derived from former monastic estates) for endowment in order to generate an income to back the loans. He complemented this original and far-sighted scheme with his educational benefactions: the foundation of St John's, Oxford (named after the patron saint of the Merchant Taylors' Company), where he installed the first like-minded, Catholic President and fellows; and his subsequent involvement in the founding of the Merchant Taylors' school. The apprentices' loan scheme was administered jointly by Bristol burgesses, St John's College and the Merchant Taylors' Company. White worked on these benefactions between 1542 and his death in 1567, establishing working relationships over the financial details, particularly with civic leaders, and involving his colleagues in the Merchant Taylors' Company; and right up until his death, 'he continued to fuss about the disposition of the college's finances and statutes'.[23]

Walter Mildmay's great enterprise grew out of his attachment to Cambridge, and in particular to his old college, Christ's (to which he had already given generously), together with his conviction that he needed to educate evangelical Protestants to go out and preach the word. This is clear from his college statutes which speak in biblical language of 'the sons of the prophets', of 'seed-plots' of theology and 'right good learning' from which those grown to maturity might be 'transplanted to all parts of the Church'.[24] To promote this Mildmay appointed a 'zealous puritan evangelist' from Christ's, Laurence Chaderton, as first Master. Mildmay's enthusiasm for his project drove him to a frenzy of effective fundraising. He set the example himself by purchasing the site, donating estates as endowment and gilding the college with magnificent plate and books. This was followed at intervals with further gifts of land and property so that by 1588 Emmanuel College was endowed with half its annual income. Meanwhile, he 'opened the purses' of government colleagues. He tapped merchants – and, indeed, widows – with Protestant leanings for gifts, small and large. He approached evangelical Protestant ministers and gentry families. He even put the

squeeze on members of the college itself. In this way was built up an
impressive endowment, through donations of cash, land or rent charges, for
scholarships, funding for the buildings, support for fellowships and gifts in
kind. During its initial 40 years roughly half the donations to Emmanuel
came from those with puritan sympathies.[25] In this way the endowment
of what soon became the largest college in Cambridge compared very
favourably with other Cambridge Tudor foundations.

Thomas Bodley was equally passionate about building his great library
and equally zealous in his fundraising activity. An Oxford scholar and
teacher, while also an international, renaissance man who had built up his
own collection of valuable books and manuscripts from friends, printers
and publishers all over Europe, Bodley was desolate about the state of his
old university library. The fourteenth-century library, supplied with money,
books and manuscripts by Humphrey, Duke of Gloucester had fallen into
decay, first through a drastic decline in the number of students, and then
through the iconoclasm of Edward VI's reign. For years Bodley dreamt
that he would restore the library. Then, in 1598, disillusioned by public
and diplomatic life, from which he withdrew, he approached the eagerly
receptive Vice-Chancellor about the realisation of this project. Bodley
worked incessantly and obsessively on it. The nucleus of the new library
was his own collection of books and manuscripts. But he badgered family,
friends, colleagues and literary contacts of all kinds for contributions in
money or kind. His brother, Laurence, also educated at Oxford and a canon
of Exeter Cathedral, induced the Dean and Chapter to transfer 81 rare
and beautiful manuscripts and incunabula. The British Consul at Aleppo
donated rare Arabic manuscripts; his counterpart in Russia provided useful
books. And so it went on. Bodley fully understood the importance of
public relations, having his project publicised far and wide and 'making the
new library ... a "fashionable charity"'.[26] He knew about publicly thanking
donors and established a visible Benefactors' Register.

As well as seeing to the fundraising, Bodley oversaw the most minute
detail. He took personal care over the detailing of the wooden benches, the
chaining of the books, the state of the ink pots and quills. More importantly
he was intricately involved in the cataloguing, classification, binding and
preservation of the collection. No doubt a thorn in the side of the first
librarian, he gave instructions that rosemary was to be rubbed on the floors
of the library which he would not have disturbed by visitors 'babbling and
trampling up and down'.[27] Worse, the poor Chief Librarian was initially
forbidden by Bodley to marry, on the basis that home life would distract
him from his professional work. Opened in 1602, the Bodleian Library

soon afterwards welcomed the monarch, James I, on an official visit. The King knighted Bodley for his visionary benefaction whereupon the founder licensed the University to hold his lands in perpetuity. Strategic visionary that he was, Bodley engineered a unique agreement with the Stationers' Hall that every member of the company should supply his library with any printed book. This set in train what became the basis for the Bodleian's enduring status as a library of legal deposit. Bodley's total absorption in the library was reflected in the terms of his will in which, to the consternation of some of his family, he left the bulk of his estate for an endowment to extend it with a third floor, detailing what he wanted in terms of furniture, fitments, books and manuscripts.

The legacies of these benefactors were monumental and enduring. These colleges and the Bodleian Library remain to this day, over four centuries later, not only important institutions in the world of higher education but part of the country's architectural heritage. In the shorter term, the growth of new foundations under the Tudors led, between about 1560 and 1640, not only to a huge growth in numbers of students but also to greater definition and cohesion of the two universities.[28] Not only did the number of students at each university greatly increase, but an even greater proportion of the student body proceeded to the BA degree in the last decades of the sixteenth century. Collegiate power was greatly enhanced – another enduring legacy – as the medieval halls and hostels were completely replaced by statutorily run colleges. These were increasingly becoming places of instruction, not just for those proceeding to a higher degree, but for what became a lower or undergraduate degree. Yet this was worked out within a framework that shaped the universities themselves. At Oxford in 1565 the matriculation statute formalised the registration of all students who were to be presented to the Vice-Chancellor by their head of house within a week of admission to the University, and they were required to take an oath both to obey the university statutes and subscribe to the XXXIX Articles. Both Oxford and Cambridge were formally established as corporate bodies by Act of Parliament in 1571.

What did these benefactors achieve in the long term? Overall, they contributed in a major way to the revitalisation of the two universities and the enlargement of their functions in English society. In the medium term, some of the new colleges did not develop quite as their founders had intended, for both religious and financial reasons. Some of White's religiously like-minded early Catholic presidents and fellows were expelled under Elizabeth for maintaining papal authority and headed off for more congenial communities on the Continent. Both he and Pope might have

been surprised at the extent to which their ultimately somewhat limited
endowment left deficits on annual collegiate expenditure which meant that
their colleges increasingly had to admit fee-paying student commoners.
These developments further increased the educational benefits for students
who were planning careers not only in the Church as lay clergy but
as secular administrators, merchants, financiers or medics. Thus these
founders – while several of them had intended to reinforce the 'right' kind
of clergy and preachers as they saw it – in effect had greatly widened the
opportunities for laymen of their own professional kind.

****

Finally, given the context of our seminar today, and in the light of current
discussion about 'new philanthropy in the twenty-first century', I would like
to underscore four characteristics of these men.

- First, five out of six of them could be called 'self-made' men.
- Second, they used their professional skills in the promotion of their
  charitable causes. And they planned strategically for the future
  of their benefaction. All college founders were deeply involved
  in creating what they hoped would be watertight statutes for the
  running of their foundations. But more than this, White used his
  business acumen to devise and follow through with an elaborate
  scheme for the endowment of loans to apprentices. Over a period
  of well over a decade, Bodley put his scholarship, international
  collector's skills and understanding of the detail of what was needed
  into creating a lasting national library.
- Third, they were imbued with a sense of duty to work for the
  benefit of their own society as a motive for their donations: duty
  to their religion, in the sense of creating institutions for the right
  kind of education of clergy and preachers; duty to their family and
  locality in facilitating their careers through education.
- Finally, in days long before the development of professional
  fundraisers, these men used thoroughly modern methods of
  fundraising to realise their visions: tapping their friends and
  colleagues for donations; and publicising their cause. I would
  suggest that Mildmay and Bodley were universal models of
  university fundraisers.

Notes

1 J. McConica, *The History of the University of Oxford*, iii: *the Collegiate University* (Oxford, 1986), ch. 1.

2 See Table 1, which shows how these men fit chronologically into the narrative of the Tudor benefactors to the two universities.

3 'For some eighteen years thereafter the Augmentations dominated the machinery of central and local government and for many years thereafter, colored the financial, judicial and administrative procedure of the state' (W. C. Richardson, *The History of the Court of Augmentations 1536–1554* (Baton Rouge, La., 1961), p. 2).

4 Pope was also a protégé of Thomas More who helped him secure an entrée to government service.

5 Petre chose to have his metropolitan home in this area in 1544, and by 1552 had purchased a large house there from the Drapers' Company for £80. This was near the mansion of Lord (Richard) Rich, Chancellor of the Court of Augmentations, who had 'collected around him, in houses in Bartholomew Close, many of the officials of the Court of Augmentations, which was no doubt a convenient arrangement' (quoted from Petre's own (London) accounts by E. G. Emmison, *Tudor Secretary: Sir William Petre at Court and Home* (1961; new edn., 1970), p. 84).

6 'The lives of men like Paulet and Mildmay, spanning the reigns and devoted to the details of administration, explain the astonishing stability and marked success of Tudor government, behind the superficial disturbances of politics' (G. R. Elton, *England under the Tudors* (3rd edn., 1991), p. 410).

7 Emmison, p. 262.

8 'Ecclesiastical courts carried it out but the Queen was the driver. Her Council might have modified her actions but did not do so because those she had chosen to be on Council were not particularly inclined to urge her to do so' (Emmison, p. 194). Thomas Pope, too, despite being a man of Catholic sympathies, had equally been content to make his career through the process of spoliation of many monastic estates and was said to have played his role in the burnings.

9 Petre's wife, Anne, declared in her will that she would die 'a true member and in the unity of the Catholic Church'. Her children, including Dorothy, founder of Wadham College, Oxford, shared her faith (Emmison, p. 292).

10 S. Bendall, C. Brooke and P. Collinson, *A History of Emmanuel College, Cambridge* (Woodbridge, 1999), p. 18.

11 C. Hopkins, *Trinity: 450 Years of an Oxford College Community* (Oxford, 2005), p. 8.

12 L. L. Ford, 'Audley, Thomas, Baron Audley of Walden (1487/8–1544)', *Oxford Dictionary of National Biography* (Oxford, 2004) <http://www.oxforddnb.com/view/article/896> [accessed 18 Jan. 2008].

13 Richardson, p. 223. This sinecure was discontinued after the 1547 reforms of the court by Mildmay.

14 Emmison, p. 273.

15 S. E. Lehmberg, *Sir Walter Mildmay and Tudor Government* (Austin, Tex., 1964) (quoted by L. L. Ford, 'Mildmay, Sir Walter (1520/21–1589)', *Oxford Dictionary of National Biography* <http://www.oxforddnb.com/view/article/18696> [accessed 18 Jan. 2008]).

16 C. S. Knighton, 'Petre, Sir William (1505/6–1572)', *Oxford Dictionary of National Biography* <http://www.oxforddnb.com/view/article/22047> [accessed 18 Jan. 2008].

17 Knighton.

18 Hopkins, p. 4.

19 Bendall, Brooke and Collinson, pp. 17, 20.

20 Ford, 'Mildmay'.

21 E.g., the statutes of St John's were modelled on those of Corpus Christi, Oxford, designed by its founder, Bishop Fox. White saw to it that places were reserved at St John's for students from various city schools (M. Davies and A. Saunders, *The History of the Merchant Taylors' Company* (2004), p. 121).

22 Hopkins, p. 22.

23 R. Tittler, 'Sir Thomas White of London: civil philanthropy and the making of the merchant-hero', in R. Tittler, *Townspeople and Nation: English Urban Experiences 1540–1640* (2001), p. 110.

24 Bendall, Brooke and Collinson, p. 24.

25 Bendall, Brooke and Collinson, pp. 33, 103ff.

26 D. Vaisey, 'The legacy of Sir Thomas Bodley', *Bodleian Library Record*, xvii (2006).

27 A. Lubran, *The Life of Sir Thomas Bodley 1544–1633* (Dorset, 1998), p. 29.

28 O. Stone, 'The educational revolution in England, 1560–1640', *Past & Present*, xxviii (1964), pp. 40–80. Stone p. 60 shows, for example, a decennial rise in Oxford matriculations from 1,268 (1578–9) to 4,179 (1630–9). See also M. H. Curtis, 'Prologue', in M. H. Curtis, *Oxford and Cambridge in Transition* (Oxford, 1959); and McConica, ch. 1.

Victorian England: the age of societies

Frank Prochaska

The Victorian jurist Sir James Stephen called nineteenth-century Britain the 'age of societies'. As he put it, 'for the cure of every sorrow ... there are patrons, vice-presidents, and secretaries. For the diffusion of every blessing ... there is a committee'.[1] Charitable societies combated a host of human ills, moral and physical, individual and social, many of them associated with the increasingly urban and industrial environment. The almsgiving and charitable bequests that helped to ameliorate poverty and scatter blessings in pre-industrial Britain did not die out, but they were inadequate to deal with the changing conditions. In the rapidly growing cities knowledge of suffering was harder to come by and it was more difficult to distinguish between real and feigned distress. The voluntary societies sought to remedy these and other problems. They intervened in the relationship between the benevolent and the needy, administered policy, encouraged new methods of fundraising and often extended their influence through the country by the use of auxiliary branches.

The array of causes assisted ranged from anti-slavery to the settlement movement, from schools to almshouses, from lying-in societies to charities for discharged prisoners. As the historian G. M. Trevelyan observed, Victorian Britain was so overrun with philanthropy that 'not even the dumb animals were left unorganized'.[2] While British campaigners pioneered various causes they also led the way in charitable organisation and fundraising; and their ideas and practices were copied and imitated abroad, not least in North America. While societies supported by subscriptions and annual donations multiplied, foundations and endowed charities were much less common. They were largely a twentieth-century development, typically pioneered in America by plutocrats like Carnegie, Rockefeller and Andrew Mellon.

In the nineteenth century, no nation on earth, not even the United States, which drew much of its charitable culture from Britain, had a more remarkable tradition of philanthropy. That Britain was a great crucible of charitable thought and action should not be surprising for it was, after all, the world's leading industrial and imperial power. Moreover, it was an era of religious revival and relatively little government interest in social legislation. The level of charitable funding in nineteenth-century Britain reflected a belief that philanthropy was a measure of the nation's standing. In 1885, *The Times* proudly reported that annual charitable receipts in London alone came to more than the national budgets of Denmark, Portugal, Sweden or the Swiss Confederation.[3]

Charitable campaigners were ubiquitous in nineteenth-century Britain, yet the Victorians sometimes questioned whether the benevolence of mankind did more good than harm. Such concerns became more pronounced in the twentieth century. In contemporary Britain, we can barely conceive of a society that boasted millions of associations providing essential services and a moral training for the citizenry, in which there were more scripture readers in the workforce than scientists. The unfashionable pieties and hierarchical values associated with nineteenth-century charity tend to alienate the secular, egalitarian mind. In an increasingly mobile and materialist age, in which culture has grown more national, indeed global, a world so richly endowed with charitable associations seems distant indeed.

Reading our secular selves into history, it is questionable whether we can fully understand the motives of the charitable in the past, even when we admire their energy and accomplishments. There has also been a lack of empathy, not least from post-war historians, who tended to treat philanthropy as of interest essentially because it anticipated or encouraged state action. For much of the twentieth century, Victorian philanthropists, like the Victorians generally, were subject to caricature. Charitable campaigners were so many Mrs. Pardiggles and Drusilla Clacks, amateurish busybodies, whose faith resembled their stockings, both ever spotless and ready to be put on at a moment's notice. Even now, contemporary charities, including those with roots in the nineteenth century, prefer to avoid associations with Victorian philanthropy, which is commonly seen as patronising and unprofessional.

Though the Victorians remain pretty unfashionable, attitudes to charity have shifted in recent decades. This is partly to do with the spiralling costs and bureaucratic inefficiencies of government provision and the need to reign in public spending. But the recent revival of charity and the emergence of a new age of entrepreneurial philanthropy has also been encouraged by the collapse of world socialism after 1989, which led to a swing in the pendulum of social perceptions. The apparent triumph of the market shifted the language of politics, reshaping the context in which charity is understood. Since 1989, charity has been elided with notions of civil society, making it more palatable to erstwhile critics. As the pendulum of social thought has started to swing back in a direction more favourable to voluntary action it is perhaps an opportune moment to take another look at nineteenth-century British philanthropy. This article can be little more than a snapshot, but one that I hope will capture something of the historical reality, which does not always confirm modern preconceptions.

****

At one end of the spectrum of giving in the nineteenth century were the great British philanthropists, who may be seen as the gilded forerunners of today's social entrepreneurs. Among them were the Cadburys, Colmans, Holloways, Morleys and Rathbones, who contributed to causes from higher education to housing, from nursing to the provision of model industrial villages. But while plutocrats contributed mightily to philanthropic enterprise, we should not assume that they typified or towered over British philanthropy. The mainstream of nineteenth-century philanthropy focused on the education of the poor and the relief of sickness and distress. For every great patron sponsoring a new college or great museum there were countless local charitable campaigners who provided essential services and a moral training for the citizenry.

We are prone to think of charity as working between classes, that is, the better off giving to the poor. This is the conventional wisdom, and it provides the standard historical model that is associated with patronising attitudes and the concept of charity as a form of paternalistic social control. But it is suggestive to think of the history of philanthropy broadly as the history of kindness. This conveys its importance at all social levels and brings it down to the level of the family, the neighbourhood and common experience. The standard definition of philanthropy, or charity, is love of one's fellow man, an inclination or action that promotes the wellbeing of others. It encompasses a neighbourly visit or a widow's mite as well as the momentous decisions of national institutions with large budgets and legislative programmes.

Clearly, much nineteenth-century charity worked between classes, not least in hospital provision and child welfare. But it also worked within classes. Think of those philanthropists who gave to nineteenth-century Oxford and Cambridge colleges, to museums and to the arts. Who benefited? When the Victorian hosiery manufacturer Samuel Morley contributed to higher education he said that he wished to provide for the sons of the middle class. For his part, the patent medicine king Thomas Holloway saw middle-class women as the principal beneficiaries of his college in Egham. The John Rylands Library in Manchester, the Walker Art Gallery in Liverpool and the Tate Gallery in London were founded as great civic institutions open to all, but who were their principal users? Such benefactions do not fit easily into the conventional model of charity as the rich helping the poor.

Individuals from the wealthier classes often found themselves dependent on charity. Indeed, charity within the privileged classes represented one of the fastest growing forms of philanthropy in the nineteenth century. In an era when occupational pensions were in their infancy and the reform of Crown pensions reduced the number of the well-connected on the government payroll, charity and self-help were essential to the maintenance of the middle class. Actors, artists, musicians, playwrights, governesses, lawyers, dentists, pharmacists, clergymen, naval and army officers, all had institutions for their support and the support of their families. By the end of the nineteenth century, the charitable yearbooks listed over 300 agencies in Britain that catered to genteel applicants, from decayed merchants to old Etonians. About 50 of these described themselves explicitly as societies for 'distressed gentlefolk'. In addition, there were hundreds of charitable convalescent and rest homes, many of them by the seaside, which catered to middle-class patients.[4]

Occupational support, class solidarity, ethnic survival and denominational renewal are critical to understanding the vitality and expansion of nineteenth-century charity, whether organised or casual. Of these, denominational renewal looms particularly large, for the taproot of charity often lay in religion and the deep-seated rivalries of the various denominations. The novelist Charlotte Yonge, a devout Anglican who taught in a Sunday school for 70 years, remarked that 'prejudices are very precious things in religious matters', by which she meant that prejudices were precious in spreading the word from a particular altar.[5]

Much nineteenth-century philanthropy had a missionary character. In the competitive atmosphere, the rival denominations worshipped themselves; and they believed it imperative to teach their children the tenets of their faith and to inculcate social discipline, if only to pass on their traditions to another generation. The Wesleyan Methodists called their schools 'the nursery of the church'.[6] The vast expansion of self-governing charity and Sunday schools in the nineteenth century should be seen in this context. Sectarian rivalry and factional politico-religious struggle beset the charity school movement from its beginnings, but gave it life. That so many poor children learned to read was in no small measure due to religious rivalry and intolerance.

Anglicans, Catholics, Jews, Congregationalists, Independents, Methodists, Wesleyan Methodists, Primitive Methodists, Baptists, Particular Baptists, Quakers, Presbyterians, Plymouth Brethren, Moravians, Mormons, Unitarians and a host of other denominations ensured their survival through self-governing voluntary associations, from schools to an array of local institutions catering to local needs. In the 1890s, there were so many sectarian visiting societies going from door to door in the East End of London that recipients of their largesse were known to change their religion from visitor to visitor. But the dissembling sometimes complained that they had to attend different church or chapel services several nights a week in exchange for benefits.

The degree to which charity saturated people's lives in the past is hard to imagine for anyone who has grown up in post-war Britain. A glimpse of the social microcosm of Rothschild Buildings in the East End, itself a part of late Victorian philanthropy, is telling. Apart from the extensive network of casual benevolence performed daily by the residents in this community, organised charities luxuriated. Run mostly by women, with the assistance of the poor in the tenements, they included: Sick Room Helps' Society, Jews' Lying-In Charity, Israelite Widows' Society, Jewish Soup Kitchen, Whitechapel Children's Care Committee, Boot Club, Clothing Club, Children's Penny Dinner Society, Ragged Schools' Union, Bare Foot Mission, Children's Country Holiday Fund, Jewish Ladies' Clothing Association, a mothers' meeting and a savings bank. As the historian of the buildings noted, this concentration of charity and thrift was to steal its way into every pore of the residents.[7]

Carrow Works in Norwich, the manufacturing centre of Colman's mustard, was a world away from the East End tenements, but it typified the way in which charitable provision often operated in provincial centres of industry. Caroline Colman, the wife of the wealthy manufacturer and Liberal MP for Norwich James Colman, set about her good works promptly upon her marriage in 1856. Guided by her religious conscience, she initiated various schools attached to the works. She provided technical classes for the men and sewing and cooking classes for the women. Through such institutions, she not only encouraged residents and employees to identify with their communities, but also supported various national charities, including the London Missionary Society and the Royal Society for the Prevention of Cruelty to Animals. This was typical of the way in which the provincial associations provided the financial wherewithal for the campaigns of larger, national societies.

Mrs. Colman overlooked few aspects of the employees' lives at Carrow Works. With her husband's encouragement she promoted the local hospital, hired sick visitors and nurses, and distributed blankets, shoes, coals, Christmas hampers and almanacs. She established a home for girls, a lending library, a school milk scheme, a mothers' meeting, a medical club, a sick benefit society, a clothing club and almshouses for pensioners. Here was virtual cradle to the grave coverage. It proved a shrewd and effective combination of charity and sound business, which in the nineteenth century were so often intertwined. As Mrs. Colman put it, her aim was 'to raise the moral as well as the commercial standing of the firm'.[8] For the Colmans and other nineteenth-century philanthropists making money and giving it away was part of a single pattern, and giving it away could be as constructive as making it. Today's social entrepreneurs and for-profit philanthropists are playing out for our time the philanthropic traditions pioneered by capitalists of earlier generations.

Charities proliferated in a prosperous nation unsettled by social change and splintered by religious, class and local allegiances. Voluntary activity contributed to the ascendancy of the middle classes, but as the example of the Rothschild Buildings suggests, it also allowed humble citizens and minorities to prosper in their own enclaves of culture and belief while preparing them for citizenship. Through self-governing associations the working classes and diverse ethnic and religious minorities, who were culturally vulnerable or politically isolated, forged a relationship with wider society. In recent years the Charity Commissioners have reported the registration of hundreds of Islamic and Muslim societies, which is in keeping with this tradition.

When thinking about working-class voluntarism historians have concentrated on the co-operative and friendly society movements.[9] The philanthropy of the poor to the poor rarely gets a mention from scholars. Yet charity was essential to survival in the makeshift economy in humble neighbourhoods. It was so extensive that Friedrich Engels declared that workers were 'more charitable' than the rich.[10] He did not seem to appreciate that the kindness of the poor to the poor worked to forestall a revolution. We should keep in mind the opinion of a Victorian cleric, who observed 'the poor breathe an atmosphere of charity. They cannot understand life without it. And it is largely this kindness of the poor to the poor which stands between our present civilisation and revolution'.[11]

The statistical information for working-class charity, while fragmentary, is suggestive. A survey of artisan and working-class families in the 1890s showed that half of them contributed funds to charity each week and about a quarter of them made donations to church or chapel.[12] Hospitals were among the charities favoured by working men and women. Well over half the income of several hospitals in the north of England came from 'workmen'.[13] Miners provided for others in South Wales.[14] In the 1890s, the Hospital Saturday Fund raised about £20,000 a year through workshop and factory collections.[15] The League of Mercy, founded in 1899, raised £600,000 from artisans, tradesmen and humble subscribers for the voluntary hospitals of London before they were nationalised in 1948.[16] Tellingly, working-class voluntarists were among those who campaigned against the National Health Service Act, largely on the grounds that they did not want bureaucrats from London running their institutions.[17]

The financial impact of working-class contributions should not be exaggerated, but contributions from the less well off did not go unnoticed. 'Poor contributions', announced a Christian magazine in 1845, 'whether we consider the proportion which they bear to the whole wealth of the givers, or their aggregate amount, are, in effect beyond all comparison the most important'.[18] Along with hospitals and Sunday schools, the foreign missions were among the most successful at extracting donations from the labouring classes. The Methodist Missionary Society raised millions of pounds from humble subscribers in the nineteenth century largely through thousands of auxiliaries and juvenile branches.[19] No matter how impoverished the Briton, the heathen overseas could be made to look more wretched.

The availability of records of wealthy institutions has distorted our understanding of the nineteenth-century charitable experience. In any study of organised charity, the contribution of the working classes is likely to be underplayed, for so much of it was informal and unrecorded, unostentatious and uncelebrated, often merging with mutual aid. But the relative dearth of evidence for organised working-class benevolence should not lead us to underestimate its extent. Such evidence as is available shows that working-class men and women established their own schools, soup kitchens, washhouses, temperance societies, Salvation Army shelters, boot and clothing clubs, servants' institutions, navvy missions, sick clubs, mothers' meetings, visiting societies and relief funds.[20] When they co-operated with their wealthier neighbours their philanthropy acted as a springboard into the existing social system.

In many charities, the labouring classes joined together with their social superiors in a common cause. The precise extent of this co-operative benevolence is impossible to measure, though the second half of the nineteenth century was probably the heyday of its institutional forms. It varied from place to place, depending on, among other things, local charitable traditions and the existence of a resident middle class. The belief in material and spiritual improvement cut across class lines and acted as a powerful incentive in bringing together volunteers from different backgrounds. Whatever one's station, contributions to philanthropic causes were a sign of that much sought after status, respectability. For those who wished to move up the social and economic ladder, contact with better off neighbours was essential. Co-operative benevolence, often kindled and extended by the poor themselves, worked to unite the nation's aspirations, contributing to social stability and a common culture.

Participation in charitable causes has always been a passport to social status and social integration, but in the nineteenth century it was also an important part of the pattern of education and leisure, especially for women and the working classes. Whether in their own neighbourhood charities or working as auxiliaries for institutions headquartered elsewhere, men and women honed a basic education and often developed skills in bookkeeping, office work, fundraising and general administration. In voluntary societies, unlike the wider world over which they had little control, individuals took decisions that had meaning for their own lives and those around them. Through contact with charitable organisation, people increased their knowledge of and interest in, among other things, the law, social work, medicine and politics.

Recreating the world of nineteenth-century charity is difficult because so many of the societies, once so familiar, are part of the lost, little-remembered voluntary culture. Many have left not a trace behind. But the more deeply one looks into the subject, the richer it becomes. In contrast with today, nineteenth-century Britain was intensely local. The array of institutions, often interrelated and mutually supportive, varied from place to place. Richly endowed with wealthy individuals and societies, London provided much of the impetus behind the national institutions, which often had branches across the country.

But aspiring citizens outside the capital put their own institutions on the map, often using charity as a means of consolidating their local influence. Cities and towns in the four distinctive nations were jealous of their autonomy and proud of their traditions. As Mr. Thornton, the northern manufacturer in Elizabeth Gaskell's novel *North and South*, declared: 'We hate to have laws made for us at a distance. We wish people would allow us to right ourselves, instead of continually meddling, with their imperfect legislation'. The leading municipal and voluntary institutions in the provinces were pre-eminent symbols of public spirit and independence. By mid century, most large towns and cities could boast of voluntary hospitals, dispensaries and infirmaries, and a host of charity schools, visiting societies, libraries, asylums, homes and orphanages, often the products of the new wealth created by industry. The local middle classes were usually in charge of the more prosperous institutions, though aristocrats and working men sometimes turned up as governors.[21]

Institutions great and small had considerable autonomy and typically operated with a minimum of interference or contractual obligation. The myriad parish societies had membership numbers that varied from under 10 to hundreds. Women were very well represented in these institutions, which reflected their high level of religious observance. In the Victorian years, women outnumbered men at Sunday services by a ratio of roughly two to one, with modest differences between the denominations and localities.[22] By that time, the contribution of women to charity, which was widely recognised and sometimes criticised, can hardly be overemphasised.[23] Those institutions serving the needs of women and children were often under female management. The charitable activity of women was a lever which they used to pry open the doors closed to them in other spheres, for in its variety it was experience applicable to just about every profession in Britain.

While the range of nineteenth-century charity was enormous, some causes received considerably more attention than others. The great missionary and Bible societies were among the largest and best-funded institutions. Voluntary hospitals, which provided for the sick poor, also saw dramatic growth, with about a thousand of them established across Britain in the nineteenth century.[24] The expansion of universities was, by contrast, modest. Unlike Americans, Britons had little passion for planting institutions of higher learning up and down the country.[25]

Charity schools and Sunday schools, on the other hand, enlisted widespread support. There were a million or so pupils registered in unendowed charity schools by 1830. In the 1880s, 19 per cent of the population of Britain, nearly six million children, were enrolled in the hundreds of thousands of Sunday schools, which met not only in churches and chapels but also in factories, barns and backrooms.[26] Charity schools and Sunday schools have the distinction of pioneering the associational

model, which was to become the bedrock of charitable organisation.
One great virtue of a voluntary association was that it could be set up
on a shoestring, which made it possible for relatively humble people to
organise. To get started, all that was needed was a room, a minute book and
a few supporters, typically neighbours who shared the same concerns or
aspirations.

****

Anglo-Saxon Protestantism, it has often been said, left a legacy of free
associations and democratic ideas that was transmitted to the modern world.
Democracy comes in different forms, and in the past it did not necessarily
mean majority rule or popular sovereignty. The Victorians assumed that
local institutions outside government control embodied self-government.
Democracy is immanent in institutions. Most charities encouraged habits
of association and may be seen as an expression of democracy in the sphere
of social and moral reform. Institutional self-government, it was argued,
not only provided a check on the mechanisms of the central state – and the
tyranny of the majority – but also guaranteed peaceful competition and
solidarity based on shared interests. As a leading Victorian cleric put it: 'We
are no friends to benevolent despotisms in this land of ours. We like to …
administer ourselves. So private charity is with us an all important agency'.[27]

Of course, not all charities were democratic and pluralist. Many
were intolerant and unaccountable, and a few run by autocrats. But as
Lord Nathan put it in his report on charity in the 1950s, most of them
served as 'nursery schools of democracy'.[28] This view is especially apt in the
context of the emergence of representative government in the nineteenth
century. For British women, who were denied the vote until after the First
World War, charitable work provided the taproot of female emancipation.
Likewise, charity contributed to the emancipation of the working classes.
As Frank Field, the former Labour Minister for Welfare Reform in the Blair
government, argued recently:

> It was in charitable societies that members learnt mutual respect, how to conduct
> debate, to compromise when making political decisions, all of which resulted
> in developing a particular character ideal for citizenship. The vote was finally
> conceded in Britain because the old political elite accepted that, by operating a
> voluntary-based welfare state, the disenfranchised showed that they were already
> democrats running democratic institutions.[29]

The scope for democratic participation is proportional to a nation's
associational life. The historian Arthur Schlesinger's belief in the central
importance of voluntary associations to American democracy applies equally
to Britain. Voluntary societies, he argued, provided the people with their

greatest school of self-government: 'Rubbing minds as well as elbows, they have been trained from youth to take common counsel, choose leaders, harmonize differences, and obey the expressed will of the majority. In mastering the associative way they have mastered the democratic way'.[30]

In highly centralised states it is easy to forget that a nation's political condition depends to a large extent on the richness of its associational life, on the myriad actions, typically unexceptional and little publicised, undertaken in local communities by self-governing charities, mutual aid societies, clubs and other institutions that operate outside the state. The fluid, instrumental traditions of voluntary association made a rigid, monopolistic political system less likely to develop in Britain. The very density of free associations, catering to all manner of maladies and aspirations, thwarted the revolutionary theorists who anticipated the collapse of the social order.[31]

A democratic process takes hold in the seemingly inefficient muddle of charitable activity. Take the practice, common among nineteenth-century British charities, of electing beneficiaries by the vote of subscribers. Such institutions, often called 'voting charities', sharpened the significance of participation and had the merit of making personal bonds between the giver and the receiver of assistance. Typically, a committee drew up a list of candidates eligible for relief, and all the subscribers then voted, each casting his or her vote proportional to the amount of his or her subscription. The practice was often criticised, but it embodied a democratic process in which negotiation and compromise were essential.[32] For many benefactors, particularly women, they were the only elections in which a vote could be cast.

Nineteenth-century associational philanthropy carried forward the ancient obligation of civic and religious duty within a commercial society, with its accent on individual autonomy. Whether conservative or radical, driven by paternalism or individualism, charitable campaigners commonly assumed that free associations gave a voice to subscribers and civic leaders and a hand up to the needy, while acting as a counterweight to government. Among the most consistent arguments in favour of charitable activity in the nineteenth century was that it promoted self-help and local independence and offered an alternative to uniform assistance and rule from London. Seen in this light, philanthropic bodies, like other voluntary associations, are 'subscriber democracies', bastions of democratic pluralism.

As Alexis de Tocqueville, the great interpreter of civic democracy, put it, charities were 'schools of citizenship', part of the process of spreading democracy. Whether middle- or working-class in character, whether ethnic or religious in makeup, associational charity diffused ideas, informed legislation, broadened political participation, raised the tone of politics and cultivated the democratic personality.[33] As nineteenth-century charitable campaigners asserted, self-governing institutions served not only as an antidote to standardising bureaucracy, but also helped to heal social divisions, for they encouraged co-operation between people from different classes at the local level. This point was better understood in nineteenth-century Britain when a sense of philanthropic duty to the community prevailed over any assertion that the deprived had a right to national assistance.

As the Victorians understood, one's view of charity is ultimately political, for it raises the thorny issue of how a society should be administered. As Christianity declined and attitudes to poverty shifted in the twentieth century, charity was thought too inefficient, patchy and precarious to cope with the level of distress. Nor were the democratic claims of voluntary institutions so compelling once representative government took hold in a culture growing ever more national in character. Charitable institutions, of course, persisted, but in the mid twentieth century they were pushed to the periphery in the debates over health and the social services. Increasingly policymakers and social theorists took the view that charity was largely irrelevant to the needs of society, at best an amenity. The use of 'do-gooder' as a term of abuse encapsulated the shift in values.

By the mid twentieth century government had taken over much that had previously fallen to the charitable services. The Victorians, in a national culture dominated by Christianity, commonly believed that poverty was ineradicable, yet they sought its amelioration through voluntary service. A century later, most Britons believed poverty could be abolished, but that responsibility for welfare provision resided in the political process. The spontaneous democracy immanent in free associations had been overtaken by representative democracy, expressed through cabinet government and bureaucratic regulation. As government expanded and the welfare state took hold, Victorian philanthropists looked increasingly dated, and began their descent into caricature as amateurish busybodies in the public mind.

The relationship between government and the people of Britain changed so dramatically in the twentieth century that we may, like the historian G. M. Young, see late Victorian Britain as an *ancien regime*.[34] In turn, the Victorians would find contemporary Britain odd and unfamiliar. In the mid nineteenth century over half the population attended church regularly. At the end of the twentieth century only eight per cent did.[35] Over the same period government took over primary responsibility for social provision, with the blessing of the churches. In a secular and statist culture, in which rights take precedence over duties, voluntary societies are no longer ubiquitous. As today's 160,000 or so registered charities suggest, Britain remains a nation of joiners. It is currently going through a charitable revival. But advocates of charity should not be too sanguine. Compared to the past Britain today cannot be called an age of societies or an age of participatory citizenship.

To the nineteenth-century mind, a decline in voluntary activity was a measure of corruption in society. As John Stuart Mill observed, a social philosophy that undermined the duties of citizenship was one in which democracy atrophied. As he, Tocqueville and other nineteenth-century social critics recognised there was a connection between voluntarism and personality. In a culture in which free associations prospered, individuals had to prove themselves resolute and responsible in their dealings with others. This was in sharp contrast to an authoritarian culture, however benign, which encouraged docility and indecisiveness in its citizens.

Whatever one thinks of the Victorians, it is worth remembering that for all their failings, they balanced order and freedom as successfully as any society in history. They held government in esteem, but expected little from it on social issues. In an era of religious commitment, limited government and strong local allegiances, social responsibility was not simply a corollary of privilege but of citizenship. The 'age of societies' reminds us that the political maturity of a country may be measured, not by the size of government, but by a polity that provides the conditions of liberty conducive to civic institutions and by what citizens willingly do for themselves and for one another.

Notes

1   Sir J. Stephen, *Essays in Ecclesiastical Biography* (2 vols., London, 1849), i, p. 382.
2   G. M. Trevelyan, *History of England* (New York and London, 1929), p. 617.
3   *The Times*, 9 January 1885.
4   For details see *Burdett's Hospitals and Charities: the Year Book of Philanthropy and Hospital Annual.*
5   C. Coleridge, *Charlotte Mary Yonge: her Life and Letters* (London, 1903) p. 161.
6   K. D. M. Snell and P. S. Ell, *Rival Jerusalems: the Geography of Victorian Religion* (Cambridge, 2000), pp. 288–9, 317–18.
7   J. White, *Rothschild Buildings: Life in an East End Tenement Block 1887–1920* (London, 1980), p. 148.
8   L. E. Stuart, *In Memoriam Caroline Colman* (Norwich, 1896), p. 56 and *passim*; see also *Carrow Works Magazine*, 1 (1907).
9   On working-class voluntarism, see G. Finlayson, *Citizen, State, and Social Welfare in Britain, 1830–1990* (Oxford, 1994).

10 F. Engels, *The Condition of the Working Class in England*, ed. W. O. Henderson and W. H. Chaloner (Oxford, 1958), pp. 102, 140.

11 W. Conybeare, *Charity of Poor to Poor* (London, 1908), p. 6.

12 *Family Budgets: Being the Income and Expenses of Twenty-Eight British Households, 1891–1894* (1896), p. 75.

13 B. Abel-Smith, *The Hospitals, 1800–1948* (London, 1964), pp. 250–1.

14 R. M. Titmuss, *Problems of Social Policy* (London, 1976), p. 67.

15 F. K. Prochaska, *Philanthropy and the Hospitals of London: the King's Fund 1897–1990* (Oxford, 1992), p. 10.

16 F. Prochaska, *Royal Bounty: the Making of a Welfare Monarchy* (New Haven and London, 1995), p. 159.

17 Prochaska, *Philanthropy and the Hospitals of London*, p. 158.

18 *The Christian Mother's Magazine*, ii (Oct., 1845), p. 640.

19 F. K. Prochaska, *Women and Philanthropy in Nineteenth-Century England* (Oxford, 1980), p. 83.

20 See F. Prochaska, *The Voluntary Impulse* (London, 1988), pp. 27–31, *passim*.

21 On the working-class contribution to the voluntary hospitals, see K. Waddington, *Charity and the London Hospitals, 1850–1898* (Woodbridge, 2000).

22 For more detailed figures on gender and religiosity, see C. Brown, *The Death of Christian Britain: Understanding Secularization 1800–2000* (London, 2001), pp. 156–61.

23 See Prochaska, *Women and Philanthropy in Nineteenth-Century England*.

24 For hospital growth, see Abel-Smith.

25 D. Owen, *English Philanthropy, 1660–1960* (Cambridge, Mass., 1964), p. 346.

26 On Sunday schools, see T. Lacqueur, *Religion and Respectability: Sunday Schools and Working-Class Culture, 1780–1850* (New Haven, Conn., 1976).

27 The Revd. A. Gurney, *Loyalty of Church and State* (London, 1872), p. 6.

28 *Committee on Charitable Trusts* (1952–3), para. 53.

29 F. Field, 'Faith, hope and charity', *The Spectator*, 4 March 2006, p. 40.

30 A. Schlesinger Jr., 'Biography of a nation of joiners', *American Historical Review*, 50 (1944), p. 24.

31 R. J. Morris, 'Clubs, societies and associations', in *The Cambridge Social History of Britain, 1750–1950*, ed. F. M. L. Thompson (3 vols., Cambridge, 1990), iii, p. 443.

32 Owen, pp. 481–2.

33 B. H. Harrison, 'Civil society by accident? Paradoxes of voluntarism and pluralism in the nineteenth and twentieth centuries', in J. Harris, *Civil Society in British History: Ideas, Identities, Institutions* (Oxford, 2003), pp. 87, 91.

34 G. M. Young, *Victorian England: Portrait of an Age* (Oxford, 1936), p. vi.

35 F. Prochaska, *Christianity and Social Service in Modern Britain: the Disinherited Spirit* (Oxford, 2006), p. 2.

Andrew Mellon: making money and giving it away[1]

David Cannadine

Between the end of the Civil War in 1865 and the onset of the Great Depression in 1929, the United States of America was increasingly regarded as the world's first 'billion dollar country', as it was fundamentally and irreversibly transformed from being an essentially agricultural nation into an industrial behemoth; indeed, into the most successful wealth-generating economy that the world has ever seen – a position which, albeit perhaps diminishingly, it still holds to this day. Among the agents and the beneficiaries of these massive changes were a group of businessmen and entrepreneurs including Andrew Carnegie, Henry Clay Frick, John D. Rockefeller, J. P. Morgan, Henry Huntington, Henry Ford – and Andrew W. Mellon. They accumulated prodigious and unprecedented fortunes, and as their names suggest, they did so both in the traditional industries of coal and iron and steel and railroads, and in the new industries associated with electricity, petro-chemicals and automobiles. To their enemies (and they had many), they were selfish, greedy, egotistical monsters, obsessed with money, hostile to the working class and indifferent to environmental pollution. But to their admirers (and, again, they had many), they were great patriots, who audaciously risked their fortunes and their reputation, who built up the economic might of the nation, and who provided jobs for millions who would otherwise have starved.

These debates and disagreements will probably never be resolved, but what cannot be denied is that the more their fortunes accumulated, the more they inclined to give them away. As Andrew Carnegie (who in many ways pioneered this phase of philanthropy) put it in his celebrated article 'The gospel of wealth' (1889), 'the man who dies rich dies disgraced'; and from the early twentieth century, rich men in the United States began to give away more money than ever before. They did so in two different and recognisable forms. One way in which they divested themselves of some of their wealth was by donating their collections of paintings, sculptures, books and other artefacts, which they had acquired during the gilded age and beyond, to what have become known as donor museums and institutions, named after the initial benefactor, and still very much bearing the imprint of his or her personality: among these are the Frick Collection in New York, the Morgan Library in the same city, the Isabella Stuart Gardiner Museum in Boston, and the Huntington Library in San Marino, California. The second way in which some of these rich men disposed of their money was by setting up foundations which were devoted to a variety of humane causes, among them the Carnegie Corporation, the Rockefeller Foundation and the Ford Foundation.

One of the greatest of this American generation of accumulators-cum-philanthropists was Andrew W. Mellon (1855–1937), whose life encompassed the whole of that phase of his country's 'billion dollar' history, and extended beyond it by a few years at each end. In terms of both making money and giving it away, he was a slower developer than most of his contemporaries: he did not become prodigiously rich until well into middle age, and he only became a philanthropist towards the very end of his life, when he carried through his scheme to establish a National Gallery of Art in Washington DC. And although his philanthropy was not uninfluenced by the two prevailing modes among his contemporaries, namely the donor museum and the foundation, his great benefaction was in some ways more unusual and more original than either of them. This is, then, in itself, a remarkable story of creative and imaginative giving, but it is all the more remarkable because, and notwithstanding the benefactions of his industrial contemporaries, Andrew Mellon came from a family in which there was no precedent for large-scale giving. In ending his life with a great act of philanthropy, he was rebelling against the stern (and selfish) injunctions of his father, Thomas Mellon, and in any account of Andrew Mellon's life and work, Thomas must assuredly be the formative influence.

Thomas Mellon was born in 1813 in County Tyrone in Ireland, where his forebears had lived since migrating there from Scotland. Like his family, he grew up a Presbyterian, and like his family and his co-religionists, he also grew up with an embattled and fortress-like view of the world. He disliked the effete, Anglican, Anglo-Irish landowning class who were his social superiors; he loathed the Catholic working class beneath him with even greater vehemence; and he disliked paying taxes, which were pressing particularly heavily in the latter stages of the Napoleonic Wars and their immediate aftermath. Along with his parents, the young Thomas Mellon turned his back on this unappealing world, and emigrated to the United States where, like many Scots-Irish Presbyterians before them, they eventually settled in western Pennsylvania. (According to one rare but favourite Presbyterian joke, when John Knox asked God to give him Scotland, he not only agreed, but threw in Northern Ireland and western Pennsylvania for good measure as well.) The Mellons were re-united with some members of their extended clan who had already settled, and they established themselves once again as farmers. But Thomas Mellon was determined to reject this life, and in so doing, he laid the foundations of the family fortune which his most gifted son, Andrew, would eventually raise to dizzying heights.

Instead of settling down to the life of a farmer, Thomas Mellon resolved to qualify as a lawyer, and to this end, he educated himself in his spare time, and eventually put himself through what would eventually become the University of Pittsburgh, from which he graduated in 1837. He subsequently opened a law office in Pittsburgh, and soon built up a thriving practice; and in 1843, he married Sarah Jane Negley, a Pittsburgh heiress with a substantial fortune. There can be no doubt that Thomas Mellon had his eye to business in marrying her (he would later describe their wedding as a 'transaction'), and he soon began to diversify his activities, branching out into lumber, real estate, coal mines and iron foundries. Thomas Mellon was a genuinely self-made man, and he was driven by the twin imperatives of 'acquisition and accumulation', as if determined to achieve the sort of impregnable security that had hitherto eluded his family. His preferred mode of business was to put up the money, while a colleague or partner would actually do the work; and this way of doing things gave him greatest pleasure when the partners were his four surviving sons, whom he determined to turn into businessmen, and who were not allowed to rebel against him as he had done against his own father. The two elder brothers, James Ross and Thomas Alexander, were set up in lumber and real estate; and it was for the two younger sons, Andrew and his brother Richard, that Thomas founded a small private bank in Pittsburgh in 1870 which was named, appropriately, T. Mellon & Sons.

The Pittsburgh household in which Andrew Mellon grew up was stern and severe, chilling and cold. Although his father was a successful lawyer and businessman, and although his marriage to Sarah Jane Negley was companionable, there was, even by the strait-laced standards of the time, a lack of warmth or spontaneity. Mellons never embraced or kissed in public;

they rarely smiled and never laughed; they were indifferent to art or music or to those luxuries that Thomas Mellon dismissed as 'artificial wants'. This was the atmosphere in which Andrew Mellon was raised, and as the surviving son who was closest to his father, he became, unsurprisingly, shy, distant and withdrawn. He unthinkingly accepted the secular precepts of his family's Presbyterianism, but faith was never important to him. 'If Andy had got religion', one of his contemporaries observed, 'he would not even have told God about it'. Yet it was Andrew Mellon who inherited his father's drive, determination and business ability to a greater extent than any of his three brothers; he would raise his father's collaborative and enabling model of business activity to Himalayan heights of success and fortune; and he would eventually use the same model when he resolved, towards the end of his life, to give much of his fortune away.

It was Andrew Mellon's good luck to grow up in a family that, thanks to his father's great efforts at self-help and at 'acquisition and accumulation', was not poor; and he also matured during that late nineteenth- and early twentieth-century period of economic transformation when the United States succeeded the United Kingdom as the foremost industrial nation in the world. As it turned out, western Pennsylvania was one of the areas where this economic revolution was most abruptly and powerfully manifest, especially in Pittsburgh itself, which was not only for a time the greatest steel-producing city in the entire world, but was also home to a dazzling array of entrepreneurial talent, including Carnegie in steel, Frick in coke, Heinz in foods, Westinghouse in electronics – and Andrew Mellon in finance. As Mellon saw it, the great opportunity for the small-scale family bank of which he took charge during the 1880s, was to expand it and to transform it into the chief (as we would now say) venture capitalist agency for the economic transformation of western Pennsylvania.

Time and again, from the 1880s to the 1910s, bright young men, with clever ideas, came to him, seeking finance for their fledgling ventures, and if Mellon was convinced, he and his brother Dick would put up the money, take shares in the businesses, and as they duly prospered, so, in turn, did 'My brother and I'. Andrew Mellon's judgement of men and of business possibilities seems to have been near-infallible, and the companies which he helped to nurture and 'grow' were among the greatest American enterprises of their time, including Alcoa, Gulf Oil, Koppers, Carborundum, McLintic Marshall and New York Shipbuilding. The result was a portfolio at once low-profile and diverse: most of the companies were privately owned, none of them bore the family name, and Mellon was unusual among his contemporaries in having interests across such a wide range of industries, straddling the old world of the nineteenth century (especially coal and steel) and the new world of the twentieth (especially petro-chemicals). Moreover, although he was a determined, audacious and successful banker, Mellon saw himself, following the business model that he had learned from his father, as being primarily an *enabler*. 'Real success in business', he once opined, 'comes from making other people successful'. And in the fullness of time, this would be the same model he adhered to as a philanthropist.

Even as an enabler in business, rather than as his own entrepreneur, Andrew Mellon made himself very successful along the way. His fortune did not grow with prodigious rapidity when he was a young man, but he was certainly, in the values of our own time, a billionaire before the First World War. He also came late to matrimony, but there the outcome was far less happy, for while his judgement of men and business was nigh-unerring, his judgement of women and love was hopeless. In 1900, at the age of forty-five, he married Nora McMullen, an Englishwoman half his age, who bore him two children, Ailsa and Paul. But she loathed Pittsburgh's prim and polluted environment, she soon fell for another man, and there was an acrimonious divorce, which was not settled until 1914. Mellon also came late to politics, leaving Pittsburgh to go to Washington in 1921 to serve as Secretary of the Treasury in the Republican administration of Warren Harding, a position he retained under Calvin Coolidge and Herbert Hoover. During the 'roaring twenties', he was much praised as the architect of a period of unprecedented prosperity, but when the Great Crash of 1929 morphed into the Great Depression of 1932, his public reputation collapsed. Meanwhile, and despite constant statements to the contrary, he remained in close touch with his banking and business interests in Pittsburgh, and the democrats came to see in him everything they loathed about the Republican ascendancy of the 1920s.

Just as Andrew Mellon came late to riches, to love and to politics (albeit with rather different outcomes in each case), so he also came late to art collecting and to philanthropy. It bears repeating that his own family background was philistine; that his father, although well read, despised paintings as 'artificial wants'; and that Pittsburgh was a grimy, polluted city most of whose inhabitants gave little attention to the higher, cultural things of life. But this was not the whole of the story: some rich Scots-Irish Presbyterian families, among them the Loughlins and the Lorimers, did collect art, albeit not imaginatively; the New York gallery Knoedler and Company opened a subsidiary branch in Pittsburgh at the turn of the century to cater to such clients; and Henry Clay Frick amassed one of the greatest collections of his day from the 1890s onwards, which (in

the manner of the prevailing taste of the time) was especially strong in
eighteenth-century British portraits and European Old Masters. Moreover,
Frick was an old friend and close business associate of Andrew Mellon,
so as one of Pittsburgh's richest men, he was hardly lacking for advice or
opportunity, should he resolve to become a serious collector.

But for most of his life, Andrew Mellon showed no such resolve. He
bought no art of any significance before he married, not least because he
had no walls of his own on which to hang it. Only when he married Nora
McMullen, and set up house with her, did he show any interest in art,
as something with which to decorate his walls; but with only a very few
exceptions, his taste was unadventurously commonplace, and his purchases
were largely confined to French genre paintings and works of the Barbizon
school. In any case, when his marriage collapsed in 1907, Mellon effectively
stopped buying, and it was only in 1917, when he moved to a grander
house in Pittsburgh, from which he planned to launch his daughter Ailsa
into society, that he began to acquire art once more. By this time, he was
not only buying through Knoedler and Company, but also through Joseph
Duveen; yet although he was a more ambitious and determined purchaser
than he had been during the years of his marriage, he continued to confine
himself to eighteenth-century British portraits and to northern European
landscapes. When he moved to Washington DC as Secretary of the Treasury,
he took a grand apartment near Dupont Circle, and he began to spend
more extensively on pictures. But he still saw himself as essentially a private
collector, acquiring pictures for his own enjoyment, and he continued to
avoid Italian Renaissance paintings, and any works on religious topics.

In 1925, Andrew Mellon celebrated his seventieth birthday. In
economic terms he was very rich, and in political terms he was very
successful, but he was neither a great collector nor a great philanthropist. He
was buying pictures more expensively than ever before, among them works
by Gainsborough, Vermeer, Lawrence and Rembrandt, but he was not a
collector on the scale of Frick or Widener or Huntington. And although
he made regular benefactions to many institutions in Pittsburgh, he was
not captivated by the activity of philanthropy, and there was no family
precedent for it. His father had given no money away for such purposes,
and when he had handed on his fortune, it had been to his own sons.
Yet despite these discouraging precedents, Mellon became much more
interested in both collecting and philanthropy from 1927 onwards, or
thereabouts. This may have been at the urging of Duveen who, with his eye
on both business and posterity, persuaded his very best clients, among them
Huntington, Frick and Gardiner, to convert their private collections into

public galleries after their deaths. But it may also have been that, having succeeded in business and in politics, he needed a new challenge for his final years.

In any event, it is clear that sometime between 1927 and 1928, Andrew Mellon began to take both collecting and philanthropy much more seriously than he had done hitherto, as he conceived the idea of founding and funding a National Gallery of Art, which would be located in Washington DC. One indication of this is that his purchases now moved into a much higher gear: he was no longer buying to decorate his own homes according to his own preferences, but to create a much more comprehensive collection which would serve as the nucleus of a great national display. In 1928, he acquired Raphael's Niccolini-Cowper Madonna through Duveen: his first major purchase of an Italian Renaissance religious painting, for a sum in excess of $800,000, which was by a substantial margin the largest amount he had spent on any picture. And in 1930–1, he acquired 21 of the Hermitage's greatest treasures, including works by Rembrandt, Van Eyck, Raphael and Botticelli, for a sum in excess of $7,000,000. These were not paintings to decorate his walls, but to be displayed in the National Gallery of Art he had now determined to create in the nation's capital.

Like most Americans of his generation, Mellon's fortune had reached its peak at the end of the 1920s, and now that he had decided on a great act of philanthropy, he could see his way clear as to how he should dispose of it, and he did so with such determination that by the time of his death in 1937, most of it had been given away. Soon after he had resolved upon the scheme for the National Gallery of Art, he also resolved to divide his fortune in roughly equal portions. He passed on almost half of it, in the form of stock in his many Mellon companies, to his children Ailsa and Paul, and also made generous provision for their progeny. And he conveyed most of the remainder of his fortune, which consisted not only of stock, but also of his still-expanding art collection, to the Andrew W. Mellon Educational and Charitable Trust, which he established to hold both the money and the art which would be the founding gift of the National Gallery of Art. For in addition to giving his pictures, it was Mellon's intention to provide money to defray the cost of the building, and also to provide an endowment which would generate sufficient income to pay the salaries of the senior officials in the gallery, and also provide an acquisitions fund.

With the Republicans' landslide defeat in November 1932 at the hands of Franklin Roosevelt, Mellon retired from public life (he had been obliged to resign as Secretary of the Treasury in March 1932, and spent the next year in London as American Ambassador to Britain), and determined to devote his remaining years to the realisation of his great gallery project. But he was a marked man during the early years of the New Deal, and with FDR's encouragement, he was prosecuted for tax evasion. The details are too complex to be gone into here, except to say that much of the argument turned on whether Mellon's gallery scheme, and thus the Educational and Charitable Trust, were bona fide. Mellon was distracted by this matter for the best part of four years, and it was only towards the end of 1936 that he was able to return to the business of the gallery. By then, he had less than a year to live, but he appointed John Russell Pope as architect, and approved the designs; he persuaded his nemesis, Roosevelt, to accept his gallery scheme in its entirety; the site to the north of the Mall was agreed upon, and ground was broken in the summer of 1937, scarcely days before Mellon died in August that year. He was subsequently exonerated from the charges of tax evasion, and the gallery was completed early in 1941, whereupon, by a final irony, it was accepted by President Roosevelt, who had recently won an unprecedented third term, on behalf of the American people.

At first glance, the means whereby Mellon disposed of his fortune for the public benefit seems to resemble the two forms of philanthropy that were commonly embraced by his contemporaries: an institution to hold and disburse money, and a gallery to display art. Yet Mellon eventually proved himself to be as original and creative a giver as he had been an original and creative accumulator. His Educational and Charitable Trust was not intended to be permanent, as was the case with the Carnegie Corporation and the Ford and Rockefeller Foundations. On the contrary, it was formed with one specific purpose in view: to hold the money and the art until the National Gallery was completed, whereupon it should be liquidated. And his gallery was conceived very differently from those which had already been established by Frick, Gardiner and Huntington: for unlike them, he did not wish it merely to display his own collection as a permanent memorial to him. On the contrary, he had provided the building, the endowment and the pictures which would form the nucleus of something much bigger, as he hoped that other great collectors would add their pictures to his.

That, in turn, helps to explain why Mellon refused to allow his gallery to bear his name, but insisted on it being named for the nation as a whole instead. To be sure, this reticence was consistent with his life-long shyness; but as usual, he also had his eye to business. As he had noticed, galleries named after the original founder-donor rarely grew, because no other collector wanted to give his or her pictures to an institution already named after someone else. But they might surely be tempted to give to *his* gallery, if it was named for the nation, and so it soon proved, as Widener and

Kress and Chester Dale soon agreed to give their pictures, and many others have followed suit since. The result has been a far greater accumulation than Mellon himself could ever have made, and also one which dwarfs the relatively limited collections on display at the Frick, the Huntington and the Gardiner. Here, then, was Mellon the creative philanthropist using the same model for giving money away that Mellon the creative banker, following the pattern established by his father, had used for accumulating it. Once again, he saw himself primarily as an enabler and as a facilitator, albeit this time for cultural rather than for industrial purposes – but still putting up the essential resources to get an enterprise started, and then leaving it to grow and develop and mature, as it has subsequently done, into one of the greatest galleries in the world. As such, the National Gallery of Art in Washington DC is the singular product of a philanthropic vision that was unique, even in an age of great philanthropy.

Had Andrew Mellon had his way, his name would have died with him, and his Educational and Charitable Trust was, eventually, liquidated as he had wished. But his son Paul, whose relation to his father was a complex and never-resolved amalgam of devotion and distance, had other ideas. To his father's regret, Paul had no wish to enter the family banks or businesses, but he eventually found satisfaction and purpose in life, both as a collector and as a philanthropist. Like his sister Ailsa, he set up his own foundation soon after his father's death, and it was these two institutions which he would eventually merge, and to which he would give the name The Andrew W. Mellon Foundation. For most people today, it is that name which proclaims Andrew Mellon's commitment to philanthropy; yet he himself had never wanted that commitment to be widely known. It is one of many ironies in the life of this strange, sad, silent man who, late in life, and against all family precedent, proved himself as clever and creative at giving money away as he had earlier been at making it.

Note

1   For a more detailed study of Andrew Mellon, and his philanthropy, see D. Cannadine, *Mellon: an American Life* (New York, 2007).

New philanthropy and the arts

Sir John Tusa

'Greed is good', said the legendary and mythical Gordon Gekko in the film *Wall Street*. If the theories and definitions of the 'new philanthropy' are to be believed, then 'Giving is good'. There is only one problem for the arts world – at least in the United Kingdom – in that the new philanthropists and the new giving are not coming their way. This is not reprehensible – individuals have a total right to spend their money as they wish – but it is sad for the arts world and should be seen as a problem to address and a challenge to overcome. I will be looking at the reasons for the gap and what might be done about it in the rest of this article.

I will summarise my understanding of the new philanthropy and the character of the new philanthropists first. The language is clear and entirely drawn from the business world where the new money has been made. According to *The Economist*, key phrases include 'social investing', 'venture philanthropy', 'social entrepreneurship' and 'leverage'. (I do wonder if these are not too oxymoronic for comfort, but perhaps the deliberate yoking together of assumed opposites is one of the intentions of the new approach.) More deeply, the new thinking contrasts 'charity' – which alleviates the symptoms of distress – with 'philanthropy' – which invests in solutions to the underlying problem. This is posed in metaphorical form as the contrast between the 'poor house and the soup kitchen' and the opposed values and outlook of 'freedom, individualism and entrepreneurism'. As one leader in the field put it to me, they want to create independence rather than dependence.

In one sense, there is nothing new about this. Think of the classic Oxfam poster saying: 'Give a man a fish and you feed him for a day. Teach a man to fish and you feed him for life.' Still the ideal is a good one and worth renewing.

The novel characteristics of this approach are that the new donors are more strategic and engaged; they focus on impact, accountability and transparency; they regard their donations as social investment, and investment expects a return; and they target gaps in the provision of current services. As the same leading figure in this field said to me, 'the new philanthropists are applying private sector solutions to the social sector'.

There is also, as Theresa Lloyd has noted, a considerable belief that 'the role of the state is to provide the basics, and the role of the philanthropist is to make the basic best'. More robustly, *The Economist* summed up the critique of the existing organisations by the new philanthropists as being that philanthropy must 'shed the remnants of amateurism' and must become a 'modern, efficient, global industry'.

In a refinement of the characteristics of new philanthropists, *Management Today* included speed of reaction; new thinking; an end to what it called 'fluffy, unfocussed and inefficient charities'; and the dictum from Arki Busson that 'it's OK to miss a target but it's not OK to keep it from your donors'. As a well-known old-ish philanthropist put it to me, 'they want to use their money, not lose it'. And he and others to whom I have spoken have said: 'there's not much fun in plugging a running resource gap or just making good an operating deficit'.

At this point, it is important to enter a reservation. New philanthropists are not better than the rest of us. And as Jon Moulton of Alchemy Partners has observed, 'some people are going out of their way to make sure their giving is not very attractive, not graceful'.

What sort of people are – typically – the new philanthropists? Based on several conversations with considerable donors to the arts, who do not define themselves as 'new philanthropists', a familiar 'np' profile would look something like this. They have created wealth out of nothing; they are self-made; they are clever; they are dirigiste by nature and outlook; they believe they have skills to offer which the charitable sector lacks or is frightened to use. In addition, they are wholly private sector oriented, and very critical of, or even hostile to, state activity, which they regard as burdensome, obstructive, slow, bureaucratic and inefficient. They are also, one of the interviewees observed, in it for the fun. Being involved is more fun than signing cheques. Though another judged that receiving serious investment-style reports was as important to them as intervention in management and operations. Again, whether this is right or wrong, good or bad, effective or ineffective, that is the new reality.

How do we in the arts make the best of it, for we have not managed to do so at present? Interestingly, the characteristics of the modern 'new philanthropist' are strikingly close to those of the sixteenth-century figures discussed by Jill Pellew – they were (and are) self-made, with keen strategic interests and significant professional skills, and are influenced by a wish to help the community, which is itself driven by a sense of duty to give something back. The sense of continuity in the motivation for giving is reassuring, suggesting something rather permanent in the entire process.

Let me at this stage introduce a very different model of giving by way of contrast. In the terms I have been discussing, this is old philanthropy sourced from what was in American terms old-ish money. But it is an example worth cherishing. The people concerned are Ken and Judy Dayton of Minneapolis, whose family wealth came from the Dayton-Hudson retail stores. Not only did the Daytons give away more than US$100 million in Ken's lifetime – Judy Dayton is still active as a huge supporter of the arts – but Ken Dayton set out a detailed philosophy of why the rich should give and how to produce the best result for the recipients and the greatest happiness for the givers.

Among Ken Dayton's Ten Principles of 'the Art of Giving' were: 'A good giver enjoys giving. He or she is happy to part with the money because you know it is going to help. For some giving is a painful and necessary act. For the good giver it is a joy.' Then: 'The good giver shouldn't be arrogant. A good giver gives freely rather than with all sorts of conditions. A good giver has faith in the institution that receives a gift.' (Do not for a moment think that the Daytons were sentimental suckers for good causes; to become one of their recipients, an organisation had to pass a rigorous good financial housekeeping test.)

Towards the end of Ken's life, he and Judy took an even more radical step. Rather than restricting themselves to giving the maximum allowable by the Internal Revenue Service, they said, 'how much can we afford to give? How much do we want to give regardless of tax deductibility?' They calculated what they personally needed to live on, how much their family should inherit, and gave the rest away. As Ken Dayton concluded: 'We have been able to share our wealth and see it at work while some have been concerned primarily with increasing their wealth.'

Now there is no good or bad about different ways of giving. There may be wise or foolish ways of giving; selfish or selfless ways. Those are decisions entirely for the giver. Though as Ken Dayton might have said, and the Bible certainly does, 'The Lord loves a cheerful giver!' And the Romans had a useful phrase on the subject: 'Bis dat qui cito dat', which you will recall means, 'He gives twice who gives quickly'. But this is not a time for judgements. All we can do is examine different models and observe how they do or do not apply to the world of the arts.

I have checked with others my own impressions of charitable support for the arts from the new philanthropists. They confirm my observation that, by and large, the arts play no part in the new philanthropy scene, and vice versa. The reasons I have been given vary somewhat, but do so around a fairly close theme. One colleague told me: 'I have not found many entrepreneurs who want to use the arts as a way of ending deprivation.' Another observed: 'The arts world is difficult to penetrate and doesn't lend itself easily to solutions. After all, you can't produce the arts to order.' A third pointed out: 'The new philanthropists love to work with the disadvantaged, ethnic minorities and urban deprivation. They're not clear how, say, supporting a symphony orchestra will achieve these ends and besides, they've been told that classical music is white and elitist.' He summed it up: 'New philanthropists are less interested in conventional, old style funding of excellence.' Excellence versus deprivation – there's a polarity.

Now you might say that those observations are interesting but hardly unexpected. One of my respondents, though, took the analysis of the problem to an altogether deeper level:

> Look – the new philanthropists are so hostile to the state that they shy away from supporting institutions that are largely funded by the state. Nor I think do they recognise that, say, museums and galleries are very mixed, multi-purpose institutions; they don't really get them. But fundamentally, why do the new philanthropists fund relief in Africa? Because they are global, not local; their money is global, not local. So they have a very poor sense of the value of support for the local.

Let me make it clear, these are perfectly valid reasons for not supporting the arts at home. Before I turn to ways in which the arts world should try to make good these views, I must state that there are aspects of the British arts scene that perhaps the new philanthropists themselves – and maybe even some older ones – do not fully understand. What are they?

First, is there a poor perception among donors of all kinds about the way arts organisations actually behave? In my own experience, I have found businessmen who were totally surprised by the professionalism within the market; by the realistic way we price according to demand; by the way we address, measure and live with risk; by the thoroughness with which we build and promote our brands; by the way different arts organisations differentiate themselves from their competitors and partners. One leading museum director said, 'we differentiate ourselves as thoroughly as the High Street'. If you consider the run of London exhibitions at the time of writing – 'The First Emperor' at the British Museum; Louise Bourgeois at Tate Modern; 'Renaissance Siena: Art for a City' at the National Gallery;

'Pop Art Portraits' at the National Portrait Gallery; 'The Golden Age of Couture' at the V&A – each show relates to the core values and purposes of the institution; by and large none of these shows would be put on by one of the others; together they represent an extraordinarily rich offering that had not come about by chance. Brand differentiation between the museums and galleries reflects their business professionalism, not amateurish accident. Many donors do not know that or give the organisations the credit they deserve.

The fundamental blockages in the way of persuading new philanthropists that the arts are fertile and effective ground for investment lie elsewhere, mainly in the apparent and perceived contradiction between relieving deprivation and fostering excellence. I say 'apparent and perceived' deliberately.

When schools in deprived areas of East London find that their academic results improve because their children take part in arts activity with organisations such as the London Symphony and the Barbican, does investment in these activities not relieve deprivation? When the creation of an arts centre such as the Sage Gateshead – to name only one – revives an entire region, creatively and economically, cannot that count as relieving deprivation? When children from the favelas of Caracas are given musical instruments and finally produce the astonishing performances that the Simon Bolivar Youth Orchestra did at the BBC Proms, who could doubt that that education programme had reduced deprivation and achieved excellence at the same time?

For while the arts should never again fall into the trap baited in the early years of New Labour, namely that they could only justify their existence by their economic, social and educational impact – a would-be Faustian pact if ever there was one – it may be that an ingredient in the essential dialogue between new philanthropy and the arts must be about the real impact on social deprivation that the arts do make. But that contribution can only be made because it is rooted in excellence in the first instance.

Other actions that the arts might take include: acknowledging donors and their generosity more; presenting opportunities for giving as an investment opportunity rather than as merely closing a funding gap; making the case for need more effectively and convincingly; finding ways of engaging social entrepreneurs in an arts organisation's strategic planning, without trespassing on or undermining the role of Trustees; demonstrating that resources are well and professionally used; and showing that the arts are risk aware, risk inclined but professionally equipped to manage the consequences of that risk.

Such an agenda might open up the beginnings of what is surely an essential new dialogue between the arts and new philanthropy. Without it, the arts miss an opportunity; but then so do the new philanthropists themselves. Are doors and minds open?

Printed in the United Kingdom
by Lightning Source UK Ltd.
130501UK00001B/85-267/P